The Sticker Treasury of Ghosts & Dark Curiosities

Smith Street Books

HALLOWE'EN

Hallowe'en

HALLOWE'EN FACES!
PERHAPS YOU WILL BE SLEEPING AND YOU'LL MISS A FUNNY SIGHT
OF EERIE FACES PEEPING FOR HALLOWE'EN'S THE NIGHT.
DESIGN COPYRIGHTED, JOHN WINSCH, 1913.

HALLOWE'EN

JOLLY HALLOWE'EN

И. БИЛИБИНЪ 1900.

Res
RAPHAEL
Rael

Conway Castle

祥邨

Halloween

A.J.D.G. 1919

И. БИЛИБИНЪ

Steinlen

G Doré

W. A. Rogers

WARWICK GOBLE

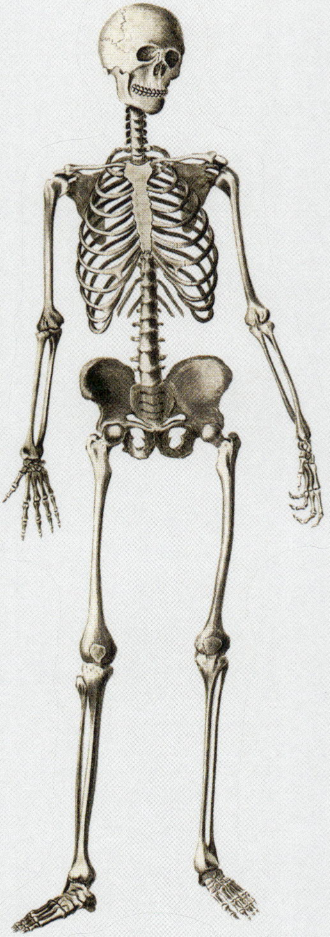

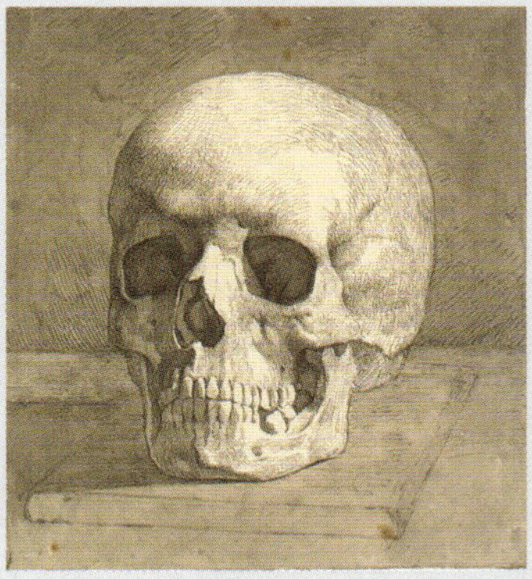

ENSOR.

SPINOZA
BIBLIA

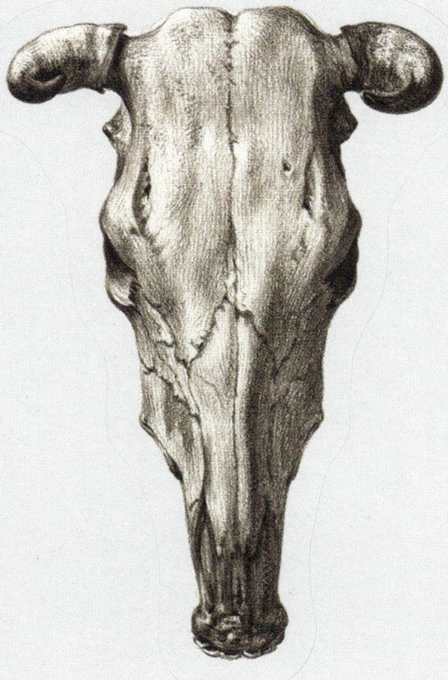

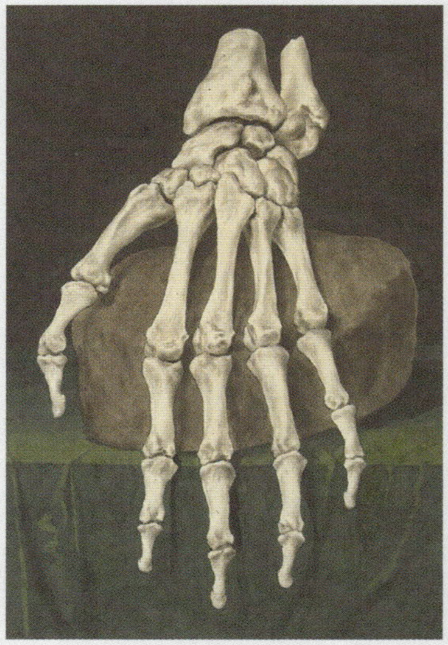

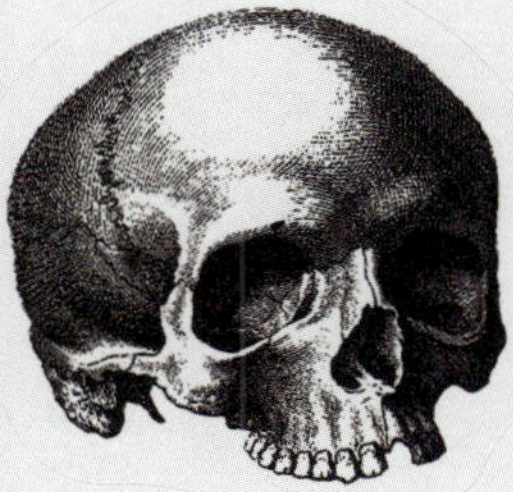
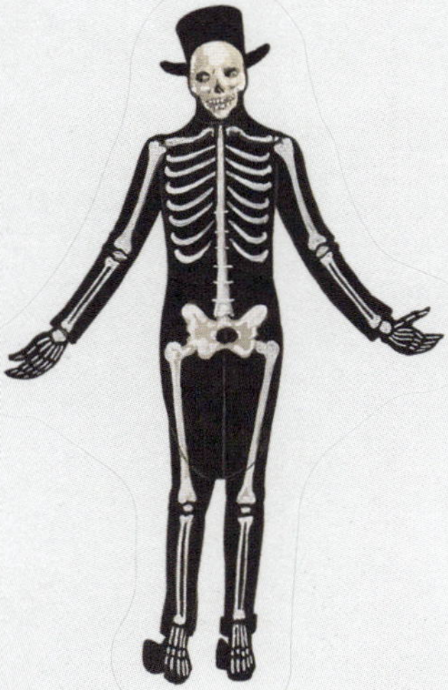
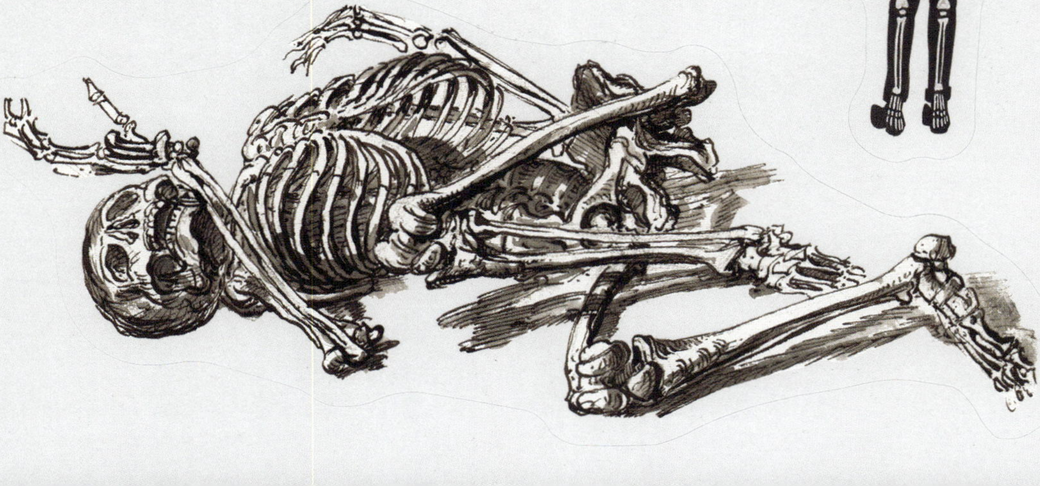

CONVERSATIO

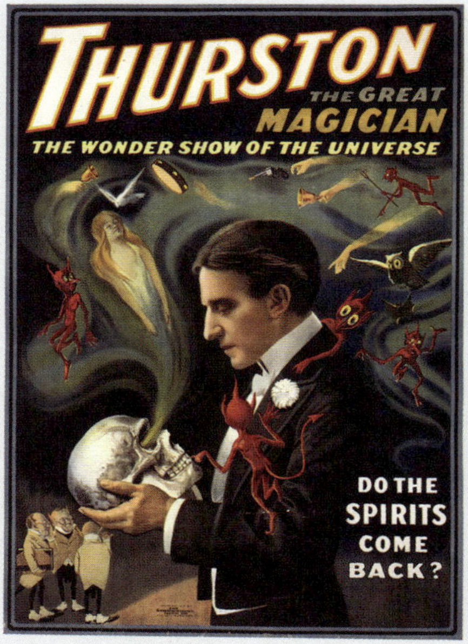
THURSTON
THE GREAT
MAGICIAN
THE WONDER SHOW OF THE UNIVERSE
DO THE
SPIRITS
COME
BACK?

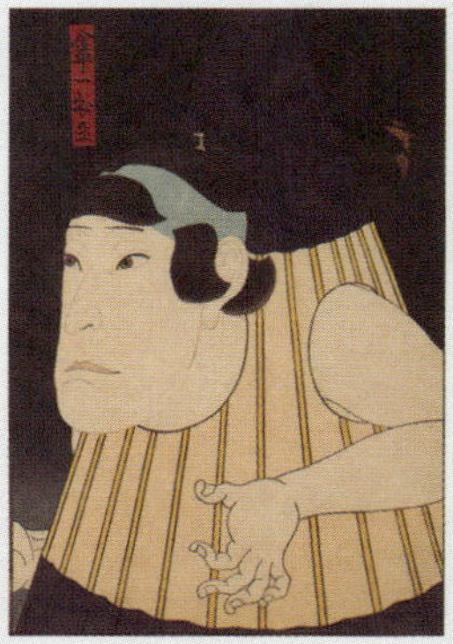

WARWICK GOBLE

F. S. COBURN

和漢百物語

W. HEATH ROBINSON

KELLAR
AND HIS
PERPLEXING CABINET
MYSTERIES

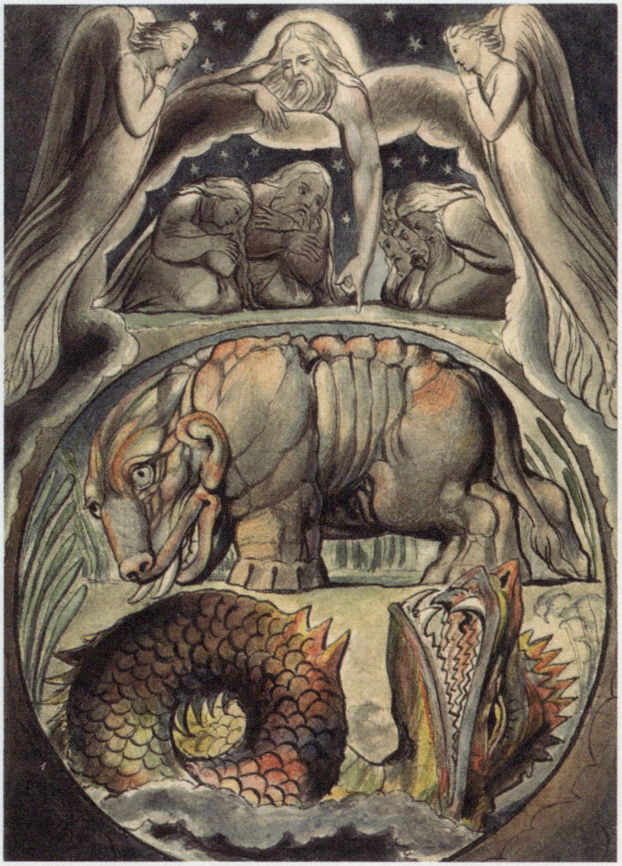

お岩さん
百物語

Deluge of Blood
WOK

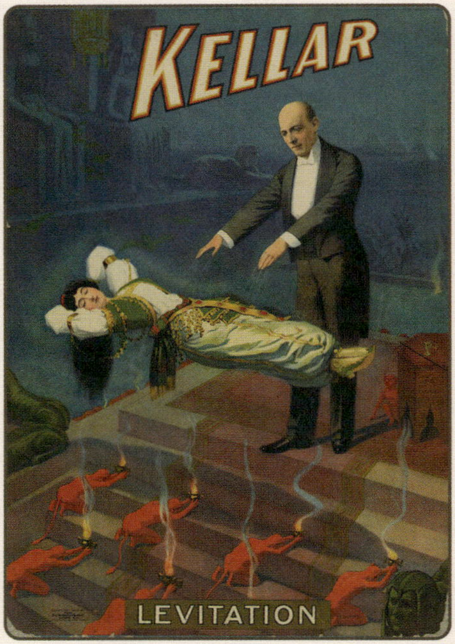
KELLAR
LEVITATION

さらやしき
百物語
前北斎筆
鶴喜板

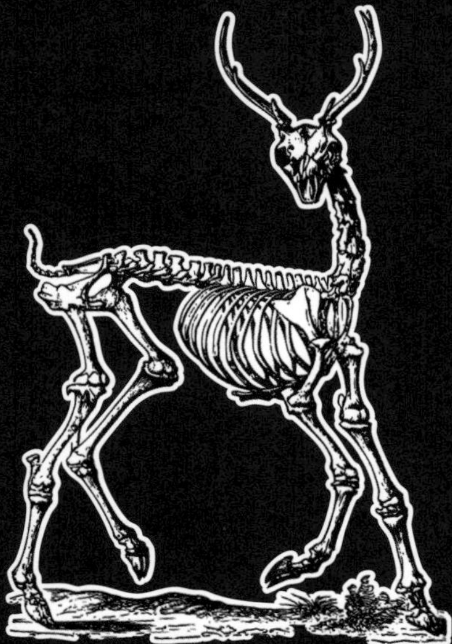

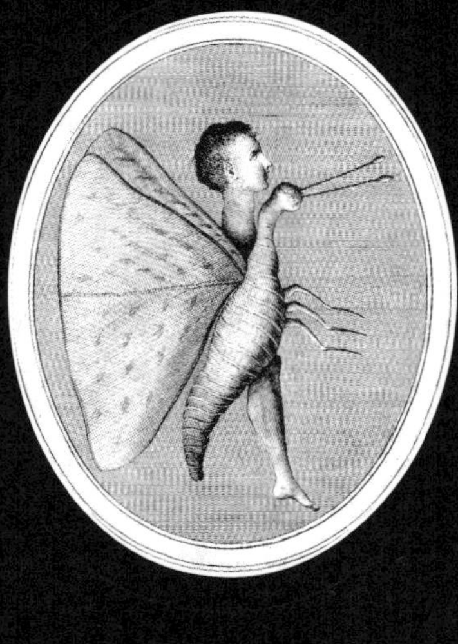

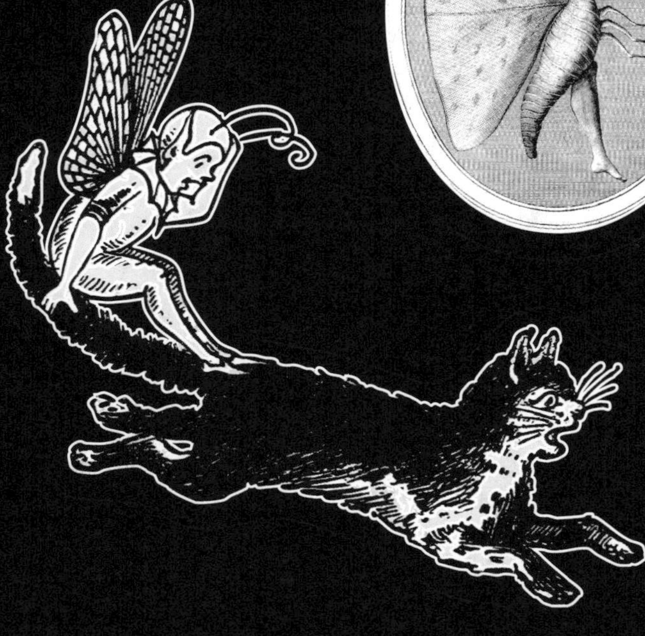

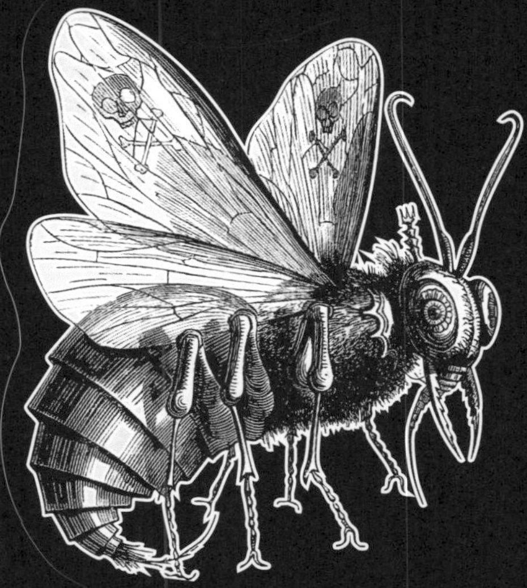

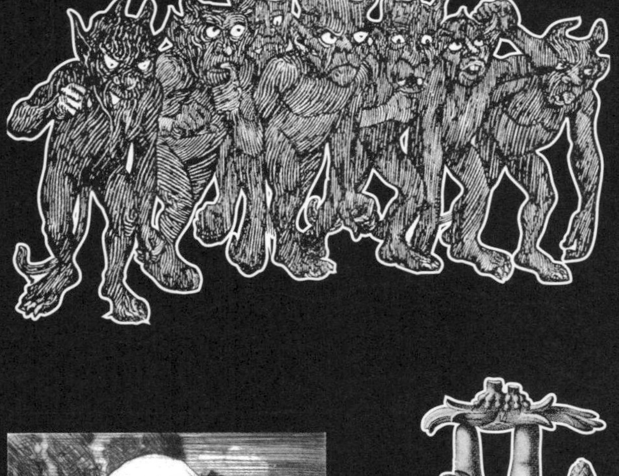

Germain
The Wizard

THE INCOMPARABLE
ALBINI
WORLDS MASTER MAGICIAN
AND ILLUSIONIST

KELLAR

HALLOWE'EN

本朝水滸傳剛勇八百人一個
鷲池平九郎
一勇斎國芳画

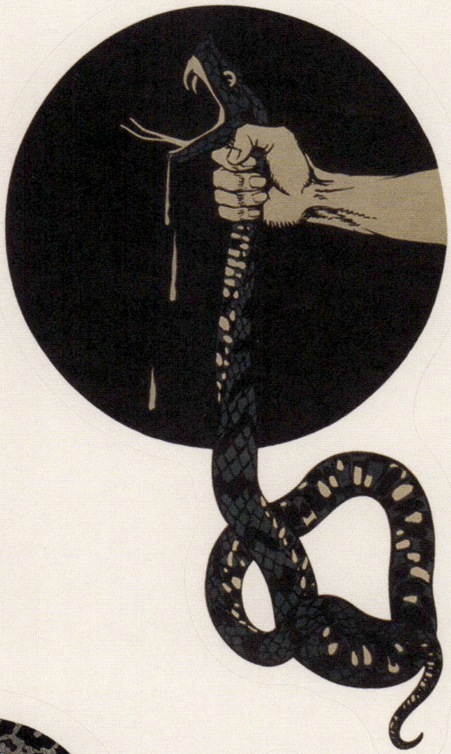

THE·RAT·RETIRED·FROM·THE·WORLD.

YAN DARGENT

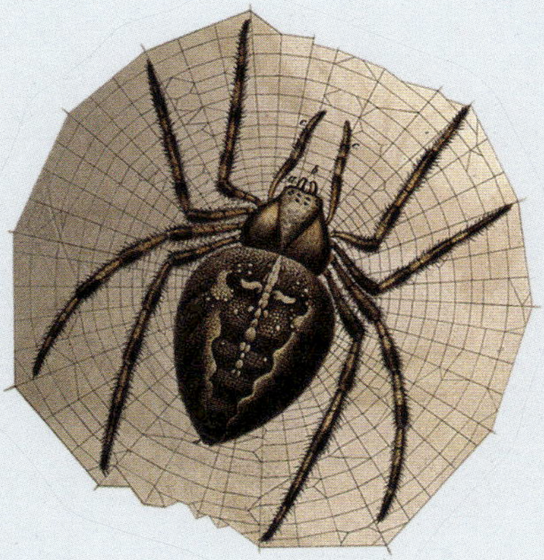

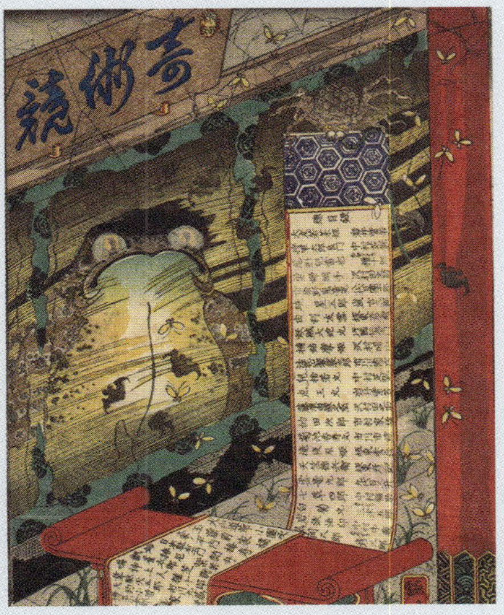
奇術競

VII.
PTEROPUS. ROUSSETTES.
1. P. edulis Edible R.
2. _ funereus Funereal
3. _ Phaeops Black-faced
4. _ chrysoproctus Golden-backed
5. _ Macklotii Macklot's
6. P. ursinus Ursine R.
7. _ Tonganus Tonga _
8. 9. _ skull & teeth _
10. _ griseus Grey _
11. 12. _ labiatus Long-lipped
Landsr. Turvey del. & sc.

KOU
KA

Published in 2025 by Smith Street Books
Naarm (Melbourne) | Australia
smithstreetbooks.com

Distributed outside of ANZ, North & Latin America by
Thames & Hudson Ltd., 6–24 Britannia Street, London, WC1X 9JD
thamesandhudson.com

EU Authorised Representative: Interart S.A.R.L.
19 rue Charles Auray, 93500 Pantin, Paris, France
productsafety@thameshudson.co.uk; www.interart.fr

ISBN: 978-1-9232-3937-1

Smith Street Books respectfully acknowledges the Wurundjeri People of the Kulin Nation, who are the Traditional Owners of the land on which we work, and we pay our respects to their Elders past and present.

Publisher: Hannah Koelmeyer
Editor: Avery Hayes
Design: Holly Dunn
Image research and layout: Heather Menzies, Studio31 Graphics
Production manager: Aisling Coughlan

Printed & bound in China by Asia Pacific Offset Ltd.

Book 405

10 9 8 7 6 5 4 3 2

MIX
Paper | Supporting responsible forestry
FSC® C012521